Copyright 2017

Table of Contents

Introduction

Insurance

Automobile Insurance

Renters and Homeowners Policy Insurance

Umbrella Insurance

Disability Insurance

Life Insurance

Summary

Additional Resources

DISCLAIMER: this book is not intended to be construed as investment advice.

To my family and friends

Introduction

This book has information on personal insurance needs for individuals and is not only helpful to the beginner, but also to the expert. This book goes into detail about the different types of insurance that are available to suit ones needs and objectives.

Automobile Insurance

Many states require automobile insurance coverage. To protect yourself, and others, you must have a plan. Below are the types of coverages available on a typical automobile policy plan:

Bodily Injury

If you hurt someone in an auto accident.

Property Damage Liability

If you damage someone else's property in an auto accident.

Uninsured Motorists Bodily Injury

If an uninsured or underinsured driver injures you or your passengers.

Uninsured Motorist Property Damage

If an uninsured or underinsured driver damages your vehicle.

Medical Expense Benefits

If you or your passengers are injured in an auto accident.

Income-Loss Benefits

If you or your passengers are injured in an auto accident and have lost income from not being able to work.

Other Than Collision

Covers damage caused by something other than another vehicle such as hail, theft, or collision with an animal.

Collision

Covers damage to your vehicle caused by impact with an object other than an animal.

Car Replacement Assistance

If your vehicle is declared a total loss, we'll pay you an additional.

Accident Forgiveness

Stop a future accident from increasing your premium. This feature applies to only one at-fault accident per policy at a time.

Transportation

Pays for a rental vehicle while yours is being repaired due to a covered loss.

Towing and Labor

Provides emergency roadside assistance (such as towing, flat tire changing and delivery of gas).

Renters and Homeowners Policy Insurance

In addition to auto insurance, one should obtain a renters or homeowners policy depending upon ones living situation. The following list some of the coverages that are covered under a homeowners insurance policy:

<u>Dwelling - Building Items</u>

For condos, dwelling means the part of the building you are responsible for, which is sometimes referred to as building items or additions and alterations. Materials used for construction such as lumber and drywall, or for finishing the interior of the property, such as electrical outlets or lighting and plumbing fixtures. The limit reflects the amount of coverage you'll have for these items if your unit is destroyed by a covered event.

Personal Belongings

Personal belongings refers to all of your belongings and household goods.

Loss of Use

This covers the necessary increase in living expenses incurred by you so that your household can maintain its normal standard of living when you are unable to live in your home as a result of a covered loss. Payment will be for the shortest time required to repair or replace the damage, or if you permanently relocate, the shortest time required for your household to settle elsewhere.

Personal Liability — Each Occurrence

Personal Liability provides protection if someone makes a claim or files a suit against you (or someone covered by the policy) for accidental bodily injury or property damage and the cost to defend any such claims or suits against you. Your limit of coverage should be high enough to protect the total value of your personal assets, including your home. Example: if someone slips and falls on your property and sues you, this coverage would protect you.

Medical Payments to Others

This coverage provides medical expenses for people other than you and your family who may be injured either on your premises or as a result of your actions away from the home. Refer to your policy documents for complete details.

Flood

Flood means any flood, surface water, waves, tidal water, overflow of a body of water, or spray from any of these, whether or not driven by wind.

Other Covered Perils

This is the amount your loss must exceed in order for your policy to begin paying for covered losses other than earthquake. Refer to your policy documents for complete details.

Wind and Hail

This is the amount that damage to your home caused by wind and hail must exceed for your policy to begin paying. For example: If you have a $1,000 deductible and hail causes $3,000 of damage to your home; your policy would pay $2,000 and you would have to pay the first $1,000. If your deductible is a percentage, it is based on your dwelling limit and will vary as this limit changes.

The following exceptions apply:

Homeowner condominiums and co-ops (deductible is based on your personal property limit)

Rental property condominiums and co-ops (deductible is based on your building items limit)

In Maryland effective October 1, 2008, the wind and hail deductible will only apply to hurricane losses.

Please note that companies that issue homeowners policies may have different coverages or different names.

Umbrella Insurance

If you have significant assets then it would be a good idea to purchase an umbrella insurance policy. Umbrella insurance is also known as extra liability insurance.

Umbrella insurances is designed to help protect and cover you from major claims and lawsuits and as a result it helps protect your assets and your future. It does this in two ways: provides additional liability coverage above the limits of your homeowners, auto, and boat.

Disability Insurance

Disability is an illness or injury, either physical or mental, which prevents you from performing your regular and customary work. Disability includes elective surgery, pregnancy, childbirth, or related medical conditions.

Although work-related disabilities are covered by workers' compensation laws, disability insurance benefits may also be paid for work-related illness or injuries under certain circumstances prescribed by law.

Life Insurance

Life insurance, is a contract between an insurance policy holder and an insurer or assurer, where the insurer promises to pay a designated beneficiary a sum of money in exchange for a premium, upon the death of an insured person.

Summary

To summarize there are many types of insurance that the individual needs to account for. Be sure that you are aware of your insurance needs depending on your needs and objectives so that you are adequately protected in case of a loss or claim.

DISCLAIMER: this book is not intended to be construed as investment advice.

ADDITIONAL RESOURCES

LINKS TO BOOKS

The Powers of Compounding Money

http://amzn.to/2wGXTJ9

The Powers of Compounding Money II

http://amzn.to/2wJmBH5

AUTHOR'S YOUTUBE CHANNELS

https://www.youtube.com/channel/UCq7uNSjONd6E8tsvErAHqNQ

https://www.youtube.com/channel/UC9xoY04t1q4whrjPjf2b0Uw

AUTHOR'S BLOGS

https://thestockmarketinvestorblog.blogspot.com

https://thestockpicker2010.blogspot.com

https://stockmarketinvestorblog.blogspot.com

https://thestockpickingblog.blogspot.com

https://thevalueinvestorblog.blogspot.com

https://personalfinancetimes.blogspot.com

https://theeconomicanalyst.blogspot.com

https://mymoneymakingtipsblog.blogspot.com

https://weightlossdecrease.blogspot.com

AUTHOR'S FACEBOOK PAGE

https://facebook.com/stock.trader.39

TWITTER

@Jrlvt

LINKS TO SUPPORT THE AUTHOR'S WORK

SHOP AT THE AMAZON LINK BELOW TO SUPPORT AUTHOR'S WORK:

https://amzn.to/2gRrd9W

MAKE A PAYPAL CONTRIBUTION TO SUPPORT AUTHOR'S WORK:

https://paypal.me/JamesLynd

PERFECT THREADS CLOTHING COMPANY

Check out the author's clothing company at the link below, you can create your very own clothing / shirts; once inside the link, just click on the "CREATE' link to get started:

https://shop.spreadshirt.com/PerfectThreads

OTHER INFORMATION

The author has a Master of Business Administration degree with a concentration in Finance from the University of Baltimore and a Bachelor of Science Degree from Virginia Tech. In addition to having interests in money, investing and wealth, the author has interests in building businesses, e-commerce, sports, travel and organic gardening.

NOTES SECTION

NOTES SECTION

END

www.ingramcontent.com/pod-product-compliance
Lightning Source LLC
Chambersburg PA
CBHW071202240526
45470CB00017B/1228